Original title:
Winter Whispers

Copyright © 2024 Swan Charm
All rights reserved.

Author: Liisi Lendorav
ISBN HARDBACK: 978-9908-1-1828-4
ISBN PAPERBACK: 978-9908-1-1829-1
ISBN EBOOK: 978-9908-1-1830-7

Ethereal Breezes

Whispers float on gentle air,
Among the trees, a dance so rare.
Leaves shimmer under moonlit grace,
As time slows down in this sacred space.

Threads of silver weave the night,
In harmony, they take their flight.
Stars twinkle, whispering dreams,
Unlocking worlds with silver beams.

The breeze carries stories untold,
Of ancient lands and treasures bold.
Through the shadows, secrets sigh,
As echoes fade into the sky.

Snowbound Soliloquy

A blanket white, so pure and deep,
In silence, winter's secrets keep.
Snowflakes twirl like dancers fair,
Painting magic in the chilly air.

Footprints trace a story slow,
In this land where cold winds blow.
Every sound is hushed and light,
As day surrenders to the night.

Fires crackle with warmth and glow,
While shadows dance in soft, white snow.
Thoughts wander in a world so bright,
In the heart of winter's twilight.

Conversations with Frost

Frosty patterns on the glass,
Nature whispers as minutes pass.
Each crystal tells a tale divine,
Of moments lost in winter's shrine.

A breath released turns into mist,
In this stillness, we coexist.
Voices echo through chilled air,
With every sigh, a fleeting prayer.

Windows frost with stories spun,
In the glow of the setting sun.
A world transformed, serene and bright,
With whispers shared this frosty night.

Glacial Serenade

In quiet realms where glaciers rest,
Nature cradles her frozen best.
Melodies flow like rivers slow,
In the heart where cool winds blow.

Each crack and creak a song of old,
Whispers of secrets waiting to unfold.
Icebergs drift in twilight's embrace,
As shadows dance in frosty grace.

Beneath the stars, a serenade,
Of ancient tales that never fade.
In the shimmer, dreams take flight,
In glacial realms, pure and bright.

Woven Dreams of Frigid Nights

In the hush of winter's grasp,
Stars twinkle, a distant laugh,
Dreams are woven, soft and light,
Under the veil of frigid night.

Whispers of frost kiss the air,
Silent thoughts, free from despair,
A blanket of snow rests so deep,
Cradling secrets that we keep.

Moonlight dances on icy streams,
Illuminates our frozen dreams,
In shadows where the cold winds sigh,
Hopes take flight, like birds that fly.

Branches bare, like fingers stretched,
Against the sky, so cold, yet etched,
In the heart where warmth resides,
With winter's breath, our spirit hides.

As dawn approaches, colors blend,
Fleeting moments, winter's end,
Woven dreams, so rich and bright,
Bringing forth a new day's light.

Allure of the Glacial Silence

In the stillness, whispers freeze,
Nature holds its breath with ease,
Crystals sparkle, glimmering bright,
In the allure of glacial night.

Mountains loom, majestic, grand,
Guardians of this frozen land,
Echoes of moments, soft and rare,
Caught in the cold, suspended air.

Every flake a tale to tell,
In frozen realms where spirits dwell,
The heart listens, quiet and wise,
To the secrets in starry skies.

Clouds drift gently, a silken sheet,
Beneath their cover, the heartbeats meet,
In solitude, we find our peace,
As glacial silence grants release.

Thus we wander, hand in hand,
Through frozen paths of this vast land,
In the stillness, we are found,
In glacial silence, love unbound.

The Weaving of Soft Snowflakes

Gentle dancers softly descend,
Whispers of winter, a silken trend.
Each flake a story, unique and bright,
Weaving a tapestry, pure and light.

They twirl in the breeze, so free, so fair,
Painting the world with a delicate air.
Silent collectors of chilly dreams,
Cloaking the earth in shimmering seams.

Under the moon, they softly gleam,
A symphony played by nature's team.
In stillness, magic graces the ground,
A serene embrace, a beauty profound.

Stories Told by the Inverted Icicles

Hanging like words from the eaves above,
Each one a tale, defensive yet love.
Silent sentinels under the sun,
Guardians of secrets, quietly spun.

Dripping in time, they shape the air,
Frozen reminders of moments rare.
Every drop a whisper, every point a muse,
In crystalline forms, their stories fuse.

As seasons dance and the sun melts near,
They sigh with warmth, a soft, sweet tear.
Icicles bow with a graceful trend,
Telling us stories that never quite end.

Respite Beneath Snowy Canopies

Under the branches where silence reigns,
A quilt of white on the meadow remains.
Whispers of winter cradle the night,
In the hush of snow, all feels just right.

Pine-laden bows form a gentle dome,
Sheltering dreams from the chill of home.
Here in this refuge, time seems to freeze,
Wrapped in the calm of the wintery breeze.

Glowing embers flicker, starlit glow,
Stories of warmth in the blanket of snow.
Respite is found in this quiet embrace,
A moment of peace, our hearts interlace.

Echoes in the Snowscape

Footsteps whisper through the white expanse,
Each crunch a note in winter's dance.
Echoes of laughter glaze the air,
Memories wrapped in frost, rare and fair.

Against the backdrop of an azure sky,
Shadows of joy and time slip by.
In the snowscape's poem, echoes ring true,
A melody woven with fresh-fallen dew.

Winds carry secrets, soft and low,
Through valleys and hills, where cold rivers flow.
Nature's symphony sings through the thaw,
Echoes of life in the winter's raw draw.

A Glimpse Through the Snow

Softly falls the winter's light,
Blanketing the earth so white.
Whispers dance on frosty air,
Nature's hush, a moment rare.

Branches draped in crystal lace,
Each flake finds its sacred place.
Footprints mark a fleeting trail,
In this realm where dreams set sail.

Silence deepens with each breath,
A tranquil pause, a hint of death.
Yet life stirs beneath the frost,
In hidden realms, not all is lost.

Glimmers shine on winter's veil,
Tiny wonders tell a tale.
In the cold, a warmth is found,
Within this white, the world unwound.

Muffled Moments

Footsteps echo soft and slow,
In the blankets of deep snow.
Words are lost in silver shrouds,
Every wanderer speaks in clouds.

Time stands still, the world stands bright,
Muffled whispers fill the night.
Each breath puffs like gentle steam,
In the stillness, hearts may dream.

Hushed reflections on the glass,
As the quiet moments pass.
Secrets linger in the cold,
Stories waiting to be told.

Crisp and clear, the air so pure,
Even silence seems to stir.
Every note, a fleeting chime,
Crafting beauty into rhyme.

Secrets Hidden in Ice

Frozen whispers in the night,
Captured dreams, a glistening sight.
Beneath the surface, stories wade,
In the silence, shadows played.

Fractured light through frozen streams,
Hides the echo of lost dreams.
Timeless tales in crystal form,
Holding warmth within the storm.

In the chill, a heartbeat stirs,
Secrets hushed like lost birds.
Nature guards these hidden threads,
As life unfolds, the ice sheds.

Each layer holds a piece of fate,
Moments frozen, held by weight.
In the thaw, we seek to find,
The stories left so near, yet blind.

The Breath of the Chill

Winter whispers on the breeze,
Softly curling through the trees.
With each breath, the world exhales,
In this dance, the spirit sails.

Chill embraces every face,
Wraps around in cold embrace.
Nature breathes a frosty sigh,
Painting textures in the sky.

Every flake, a fleeting kiss,
Creating moments full of bliss.
Layers form, a tale unfolds,
In the stillness, life beholds.

As the breath of winter glows,
Life is shaped by where it goes.
In the cold, a warmth will creep,
In this hush, the world's asleep.

Beneath the Whispering Snow

Softly falls the winter's white,
Blanketing the world in light.
Trees adorned in crystal glaze,
Nature's beauty, a quiet praise.

Footsteps hush in frosty air,
Every sound both rare and fair.
Whispers dance upon the breeze,
Carrying secrets through the trees.

Beneath the snow, pure dreams ignite,
Silent wishes, hearts take flight.
In this calm, we find our peace,
Endless wonder, time's release.

Moonlight bathes the silent ground,
Magic wraps the space around.
Stars above begin to glow,
Guiding souls where calm winds blow.

Winter's breath, a gentle sigh,
Nurturing the world nearby.
Underneath this quilt of white,
Hope awakens in the night.

Reflections in a Frostbound World

In the stillness, shadows gleam,
Mirrored ice where sunbeams dream.
Nature holds a crystal lens,
Showcasing where the light descends.

Frozen lakes like glassy seas,
Whispers float upon the breeze.
Every branch a work of art,
Winter's touch, a brand new start.

Footprints mark the journey made,
Through this sparkling, chill cascade.
Moments layered, time's embrace,
Crafting memories in this space.

Colors shift in dusk's soft glow,
Whispers of a tale to sow.
Reflections spark a silent thought,
In the frost, life battles wrought.

Echoes of the day remain,
Captured in the fleeting grain.
Frostbound wonders, still and bright,
Guard our dreams throughout the night.

Radiance of Winter's Embrace

A tapestry of white unfolds,
Stories whispered, life retold.
Glistening branches, diamonds shine,
Radiance of winter's divine.

In the heart of crisp, cold days,
Sunlight finds its tender ways.
Glimmers dance on frosted air,
Every moment, pure and rare.

Snowflakes twirl, a ballet light,
Nature's brush, so soft and white.
Upon the ground they gently lay,
Kissing earth in sweet dismay.

Within the quiet, dreams arise,
Cradled 'neath the pale blue skies.
Winter's heart, both fierce and mild,
Cocooning us, the world's own child.

With every breath, the chill invites,
Magic woven through the nights.
In this embrace, between the cold,
A warmth emerges, brave and bold.

Emotions Chiseled in Ice

Beneath the surface, feelings flow,
Chiseling the heart in snow.
Frozen tears in silence gleam,
Memories swirl like winter's dream.

Every shard, a tale to tell,
Echoes of the past do dwell.
In the crystal, stories traced,
Marking moments, time embraced.

Through the storms, our spirits fight,
Each emotion carved in light.
Resilience held in icy grip,
Navigating every slip.

In the cold, we learn to stand,
Facing life, hand in hand.
Every heartbeat, strong and true,
A testament, born anew.

Emotions shaped by nature's art,
Carved in ice, yet warm the heart.
Within the chill, we find our place,
Embracing life, with tender grace.

Specters of Light in Glistening White

In the hush of winter's glow,
Specters dance in moonlit snow.
Glistening white, a tranquil sight,
Whispers echo through the night.

Stars weave tales in silver threads,
Where the heart of silence treads.
Floating softly, dreams take flight,
Chased by shadows, kissed by light.

Branches hold the frosty dew,
While the world seems fresh and new.
Each breath paints the air with grace,
Time slows down in this embrace.

The stillness sings of peace profound,
In the beauty all around.
Nature's splendor, pure delight,
Wrapped in specters, glowing bright.

As dawn approaches, whispers fade,
Morning's hues begin to wade.
Yet the memory lingers tight,
Of the specters, glistening white.

The Calm of Frosted Trees

Frosted boughs in morning light,
Rest upon the world so bright.
Nature holds a breath so deep,
In this quiet, dreams will sleep.

Snowflakes settle, soft and small,
Blanket everything with a shawl.
Whispers of the chill that freeze,
Calmly coat the ancient trees.

Birds are hushed, their songs on hold,
In the beauty, pure and bold.
Stillness reigns, a sacred space,
Time suspended, a soft embrace.

Every branch a work of art,
Crafted by the winter's heart.
In this realm where spirits please,
Find your peace among the trees.

As sunlight breaks, the shadows play,
Chasing dreams of yesterday.
Yet the calm, it always stays,
In the frost of winter's gaze.

Twilight's Soft Embrace

Twilight drapes the world in hues,
Whispers secrets to the blues.
Softly comes the evening sigh,
As the day begins to die.

Stars awaken, one by one,
Painting stories, dreams begun.
In the dusk, the shadows blend,
Time to pause, to softly mend.

Moonlight glimmers on the lake,
Rippling gently, ripples wake.
Every heartbeat sings so clear,
Twilight's touch, so warm, so near.

Gentle breezes start to weave,
Through the branches, as they grieve.
Yet there's beauty in their fall,
In Twilight's arms, we find it all.

As the night enfolds the land,
Hold this moment, close your hand.
In the stillness, find your grace,
In the twilight's soft embrace.

Tapestry of Snowy Silence

In the quiet blanket lay,
Winter's hush holds night at bay.
Every flake, a whispered plea,
Woven into harmony.

Softly falls the snow so pure,
Nature's magic, ever sure.
Crafting scenes of peaceful white,
In the depths of winter's night.

Footsteps muffled, silence deep,
In this moment, we can leap.
Into dreams that gently rise,
Beneath the darkening skies.

Each branch bends with crystal bliss,
Wrapped in winter's tender kiss.
Every heartbeat, every breath,
Whispers tales of life and death.

Through the night, the stars align,
In the beauty, still, we shine.
Tapestry of snowy hue,
Wrapping all in peace anew.

Echoes of the Cold

Whispers dance in frosted air,
Footsteps crunch on icy ground.
Shadows linger, none to care,
Silent beauty all around.

Glistening branches, pale and neat,
Nature's artwork crafted fine.
Breath of winter, sharp and sweet,
Time does pause, a quiet sign.

Fires crackle, warmth in sight,
Echoes of the cold embrace.
Hearts grow closer in the night,
Finding solace in this space.

Daylight wanes, the stars ignite,
Moonlight weaves a silver thread.
In the velvet cloak of night,
All the whispered dreams are spread.

Voices softly intertwine,
In the hush of falling snow.
In this moment, pure, divine,
Time forgets its rush and flow.

Beneath the Silver Veil

Softly falls the silver sheen,
Blanketing the world in white.
Gentle flakes, a tranquil scene,
Whispers wrapped in shimmers bright.

Beneath the veil, the silence stays,
Crystals gleam on branches bare.
Lost in this, the heart obeys,
Finding peace within the air.

Footprints tracing paths yet known,
Curved and bending with the breeze.
Every step feels like a throne,
Crowned by nature's timeless ease.

Echoes of the night remain,
While the world in slumber lies.
In the stillness, feel the pain,
Healed beneath the starlit skies.

Whispered secrets softly call,
In the silence, hear them clear.
Beneath the silver veil, we fall,
Into dreams we hold so dear.

Shivering Silence

In the hush of winter's breath,
Stillness grips the frozen land.
Shivering silence, dance of death,
Nature waits, a quiet hand.

Branches bow to heavy loads,
Crystal crowns on every tree.
Through this peace, the heart explodes,
Yearning for what used to be.

Frosted windows, glinting bright,
Casting shadows on the floor.
Within the still and starry night,
Echoes linger, evermore.

Snowflakes fall like whispered dreams,
Each a story yet untold.
In the quiet, so it seems,
Life and love are still as gold.

Dancing through this icy veil,
Memories of warmth abide.
In shivering silence, we hail,
Winter's beauty, bittersweet pride.

Whispers in the White

Snowflakes drift on whispers light,
Carrying the dreams of night.
Silence drapes the world in white,
As we bask in winter's might.

Voices echo through the trees,
Murmurs lost in chilly air.
Dancing whispers in the breeze,
Tales of beauty, free from care.

Frosty breath upon our cheeks,
Sparkling jewels in moonlit glow.
Nature speaks in gentle peaks,
In the night, the magic flows.

Underneath the starry dome,
Every moment feels so right.
In this space, we find our home,
Wrapped in whispers, pure delight.

As the winter night grows old,
Still we listen, hearts ignite.
In these tales forever told,
We find warmth within the white.

Night's Gentle Breath

The moon whispers soft and clear,
Stars twinkle like dreams near.
Night wraps the world in a shroud,
Silent secrets, unbowed.

In the stillness, shadows glide,
As the calm takes winter's ride.
Breath of night, cool and light,
Promises of dawn's delight.

With each sigh, the darkness sways,
Painting peace in gentle ways.
Tales of old within the dark,
Echoed in the night's stark.

Crickets sing a lullaby,
While the stars wink from high.
In the deep, where dreams take flight,
Night's gentle breath, pure and bright.

Awakened souls drift in space,
Floating in a slow embrace.
Wrapped in night, we find our rest,
In the shadows, we are blessed.

Soft Shadows of Frost

Morning light casts a glow,
On the ground where frost will show.
Soft shadows dance and play,
Gleaming white, a cold ballet.

Each blade of grass, a crystal weave,
Nature's art, so hard to believe.
The chill wraps round in tender care,
Whispering secrets hidden there.

Silence reigns in the crisp air,
Every breath, a puff of dare.
In the stillness, beauty lies,
Reflecting dreams beneath the skies.

Frosty patterns, intricate lace,
Embrace the world with icy grace.
In this moment, find the peace,
As winter's wonders never cease.

Underneath, the earth will sleep,
In the frosty shadows deep.
Pondering what warmth will bring,
As the chill prepares to sing.

The Heart of Winter

Snowflakes swirl in silent dance,
In winter's grasp, we take our chance.
Eyes aglow with frosted light,
Finding joy in the crisp white.

Branches heavy, bows so low,
Nature's beauty wrapped in snow.
In the cold, we seek warmth still,
In every heart, a quiet thrill.

Fires crackle, stories told,
Laughter shared, a warmth to hold.
In winter's heart, love shines bright,
Against the backdrop of the night.

While the world sleeps, dreams ignite,
In slumber's arms, we find delight.
The heart beats on, despite the freeze,
Winter's breath, a gentle tease.

From snowy peaks to valleys deep,
Every secret winter keeps.
In the stillness, life unfolds,
The heart of winter, purest gold.

Pearls of Ice

Glistening drops on branches hang,
Nature's jewels, a soft clang.
Each pearl of ice, a story sighs,
Underneath the gray, blue skies.

Between the trees, the shimmer plays,
In the light of golden rays.
Fragile beauty, a fleeting touch,
Reminding us we matter much.

Whispers echo, crisp and clear,
As winter's breath draws us near.
Treasures found in the chill of air,
In the quiet moments we share.

With every step on frosted ground,
A symphony of silence found.
Pearls of ice, a wondrous gaze,
Forever captured in winter's maze.

Seasons change, but memories stay,
In sparkling frost, they dance and play.
Embrace the chill, find the light,
In pearls of ice, hearts take flight.

A Journey Through Frosted Memories

In the quiet of winter's hold,
Footprints whisper tales untold,
Each breath a fog, softly laid,
In the stillness, dreams cascade.

Time drifts like flakes in the air,
Memories dance without a care,
The world a canvas, pure and white,
Colors fade in the fading light.

Echoes of laughter linger near,
Frozen moments, crystal clear,
Chasing the twilight, we engage,
With every step, we turn a page.

Hearts wrapped warmly, side by side,
In this realm, where dreams abide,
Frosted paths we dare to roam,
Finding warmth in a fleeting home.

As the sun dips low and grey,
Daylight fades, but dreams will stay,
In our souls, each flake, a sigh,
A journey etched beneath the sky.

Chasing Shadows in the Snow

Beneath the pale and silver glow,
We dart through fields of glistening snow,
Casting shadows in the fray,
Lost in a game, we dance and play.

The crunching sound beneath our feet,
Echoes of laughter, bittersweet,
With every leap, our spirits soar,
Chasing shadows, forevermore.

Whispers of winter tug at our heart,
A fleeting moment, a work of art,
Time stands still in the frosted air,
Chasing shadows, without a care.

Branches bare, the world asleep,
In the silence, secrets we keep,
A tapestry woven in white and grey,
Capturing dreams that fade away.

With every sunset, new tales unfold,
Adventure calls in the bitter cold,
Hand in hand, we carve our way,
Through the shadows, forever sway.

Enchanted by Icy Silence

In a world wrapped in winter's calm,
Silence weaves a soothing balm,
Icicles hang like crystal dreams,
Shimmering softly in gentle beams.

Snowflakes fall, a delicate sigh,
Each one unique, as time drifts by,
Wrapped in peace, a sacred trance,
In icy silence, we find our chance.

The horizon blushes under dusk,
Wrapped in a golden, fleeting husk,
Whispers of dusk, so sweetly spun,
In this moment, we are one.

Footsteps echo, a fleeting sound,
In the quiet, where peace is found,
An enchanted dance, a loving grace,
In winter's arms, we find our place.

Through the night, the stars ignite,
Guiding our dreams with gentle light,
In icy silence, we're drawn near,
Lost in the magic, held so dear.

Frost's Gentle Embrace

Under the cloak of winter's air,
Frosted whispers weave everywhere,
Nights adorned with silver lace,
Wrapped in nature's soft embrace.

Each breath a cloud, fleetingly bright,
The moon reflects on double night,
Through trees adorned in icy gleam,
In this moment, we dare to dream.

Branches bow under frosted weight,
Creating wonders that captivate,
Stories unfold in the chilly breeze,
Under the sigh of frozen trees.

With every touch, the world grows still,
Time feels magic, time feels thrill,
In this season, bright and clear,
Frost's embrace draws us near.

As dawn approaches, shadows play,
Colors awaken, kiss away gray,
In the freshness, warmth we trace,
Forever held in frost's embrace.

Stillness Beneath the Frozen Sky

The world is draped in white,
A blanket soft, pure as light.
Whispers of a frosty breeze,
Carrying secrets through the trees.

Footsteps hush, the silence grows,
In this realm where stillness flows.
The stars above flicker and gleam,
Beneath the moon's soft, silver beam.

Icicles hang like frozen tears,
Marking time through fleeting years.
Nature holds her breath in peace,
In this moment, all troubles cease.

A quiet hush wraps round the night,
As shadows dance in pale moonlight.
Frozen lakes mirror the skies,
Where dreams and reflections arise.

Here beneath the frozen dome,
In this stillness, we make our home.
A sanctuary carved by frost,
In this beauty, we find what's lost.

The Quiet Strength of Winter's Heart

Beneath the frost, life lingers still,
In each frozen breath, a hidden thrill.
Branches bare, yet strong they stand,
Guarding secrets of this land.

The trees don cloaks of snowy white,
In their silence, a pure delight.
Roots embrace the frozen ground,
In winter's heart, strength is found.

The chill in the air speaks loud and clear,
But within the cold, hope draws near.
A subtle warmth begins to bloom,
In the blackened earth, dispelling gloom.

Snowflakes dance on winter's breath,
A celebration of life and death.
Through the stillness, stories unfold,
In every whisper, courage bold.

So here we learn from nature's way,
Strength in silence, bright as day.
In winter's grip, we find our part,
Embracing the quiet strength of heart.

Elysian Dreams in Cold Light

In the dawn's soft, icy glow,
Whispers of the past still flow.
Each breath a vision, each sigh a song,
As winter wraps us, where we belong.

The sun arises, golden bright,
Chasing shadows from the night.
A tapestry woven of frost and dew,
In this chilly realm, dreams feel new.

The air is crisp, the landscape fair,
Elysian gardens, beyond compare.
Within the stillness, magic hides,
Where the spirit of winter abides.

Footprints lead to worlds unseen,
In the hush, we slip in between.
A journey painted in white and blue,
Find joy in dreams, let the heart renew.

So linger here, where love entwines,
In winter's heart, the sun still shines.
Elysian dreams bid us to stay,
In this tranquil, cold ballet.

Tales from the Silent Woods

In the woods where silence reigns,
Whispers carry through the plains.
Every tree holds a story dear,
Echoes of laughter, echoes of fear.

Branches creak under the weight,
Of memories forged, sealed by fate.
In the stillness, shadows play,
Tales woven in twilight's sway.

Snow blankets paths, secrets kept,
In the hush, the forest wept.
Each flake a part of nature's lore,
Guarding tales of those before.

The nightingale sings her lullaby,
Underneath the vast, starry sky.
With every note, a heart takes flight,
In the silent woods, dreams ignite.

So walk with me, through trees unbent,
Where echoes fade, but hearts content.
In this quiet, let memories flow,
Tales from the woods where spirits glow.

The Breath of Chilling Breezes

Winter whispers soft and low,
As chilling breezes start to blow.
Nature wrapped in frosty lace,
Silent nights, a tranquil space.

Trees stand tall with branches bare,
Crystals glisten in the air.
Footprints trace where shadows creep,
In the stillness, dreams do seep.

Moonlight glows on icy streams,
Casting spells of silver dreams.
With every gust, the world awakes,
In the quiet, peace it makes.

Stars twinkle in the frigid sky,
Glistening gems as time flows by.
Breath of winter, crisp and clear,
In this season, calm is near.

Embrace the chill, a gentle sigh,
The breath of breezes, a soft cry.
Nature's heart begins to cease,
In this silence, find your peace.

Hushed Murmurs Beneath the Snow

Beneath the snow, a whisper calls,
Hushed murmurs in silent halls.
Nature sleeps, a gentle shroud,
Wrapped in white, a tranquil crowd.

Frozen branches lightly sway,
Softly greeting winter's day.
Footsteps leave a fleeting trace,
In the snow, a quiet grace.

Echoes of the wind's embrace,
Songs of peace in this still space.
Hushed murmurs of the earth's own breath,
In snow's blanket, life finds death.

Soft snowflakes dance from skies above,
Each a token of nature's love.
The world is wrapped in gentle dreams,
Where everything's more than it seems.

Beneath the white, new life will rise,
As winter fades, the sun will prize.
Hushed whispers turn to joy and cheer,
Awakening the springtime near.

Crystal-Laden Dreams

In the realm of crystal gleams,
Woven webs of silent dreams.
Every flake a tale to tell,
Where magic and the shadows dwell.

Icicles hanging from the eaves,
Shimmering light in frosty leaves.
Whispers of a winter night,
Hold the heart in pure delight.

Glistening paths in silver spun,
Underneath the frosted sun.
Each step echoes soft and sweet,
Crystals glimmer beneath our feet.

Dreams take flight on wings of light,
In the silence, hearts feel right.
Finding solace, pure and clear,
In this mosaic, winter's cheer.

A sparkling world, a fleeting scene,
In the frost, the life unseen.
Crystal-laden hopes arise,
Beneath the ever-watching skies.

Twilight's Frostfire

As twilight drapes the world in blue,
Frostfire glimmers with every hue.
The sun bids night a warm farewell,
In the chill, its secrets swell.

Embers dance on the frosty air,
Painting stories, beyond compare.
Whisps of smoke in colors bright,
Merging dreams with coming night.

Softly now, the shadows creep,
As the land prepares for sleep.
Frostfire glows, a fleeting light,
In the calm of the end of night.

Stars awaken, twinkling high,
Painting the vast and velvet sky.
A symphony of frost and fire,
In the stillness, hearts aspire.

Twilight sings its gentle song,
In the dark, where dreams belong.
Frostfire flickers, warm and bright,
Welcoming the magic of night.

Midnight's Icy Embrace

Under the veil of stars so bright,
Midnight whispers in the frozen night.
Shadows dance on the glimmering frost,
In the stillness, nothing is lost.

Crystals form on the windowpane,
A silent song in the winter's reign.
Chill winds weave through the ancient trees,
Carrying secrets on the icy breeze.

Moonlight glistens on the ground below,
Painting paths in silver and snow.
Every breath hangs in the shimmering air,
A moment captured, fragile and rare.

As dreams flutter like leaves in the dark,
Caught in the night's enchanting spark.
Wrapped in tranquility's soft embrace,
Time stands still in this frozen space.

The hour glows with a haunting pride,
Where echoes of whispers softly bide.
In midnight's arms, the world seems new,
Bathed in the calm of a frost-kissed hue.

The Quiet of Falling Snow

In the hush of a whispering eve,
Soft snowflakes begin to weave.
Each flake dances to the ground,
Wrapping the world in silence profound.

Blankets of white grace every tree,
A peaceful moment, wild and free.
Gentle drifts cover paths and stones,
In their softness, the heart atones.

Stillness reigns as time slows down,
Silvery coats on each sleepy town.
Nature holds her breath with care,
In this magic, we lose despair.

Frosty breezes kiss the air,
Inviting warmth in every stare.
Under the glow of streetlight's beam,
The landscape echoes a tranquil dream.

With every flake, a promise made,
In winter's grasp, worries fade.
Together we find solace here,
In the quiet of snow, everything is clear.

Frosty Tides of Time

Upon the shores where shadows creep,
Frosty tides in silence sweep.
Waves of time, both cruel and kind,
Carry whispers of the mind.

Each ripple maps the journey carved,
In icy depths, our hopes preserved.
Moments captured in frosted glass,
Eternal echoes of days that pass.

Silvery mirrors reflect the sky,
Where dreams drift like a distant sigh.
Seagulls cry in the biting wind,
As time meanders, unaware of sin.

Under the moon's cold, watchful gaze,
Life unfolds in a frozen haze.
With every tide that claims the shore,
We learn to let go, to seek for more.

In the chill of night, we reminisce,
Of fleeting moments and gentle bliss.
Frosty tides shape the sands of fate,
In their embrace, we learn to wait.

Glistening Footprints

On a path where snowflakes play,
Footprints glisten, marking the way.
Each step tells a story bold,
Of journeys new and adventures untold.

In the shimmering blanket white,
Memories dance in morning light.
Echoes linger in the frosty air,
Of laughter shared without a care.

From the forest's edge to hills so high,
Trails lead onward, beneath the sky.
Every imprint a trace of the past,
In winter's grip, none are lost, none cast.

Stars may twinkle in a velvet night,
Guiding our steps till the dawn's first light.
In this magic, we find our way,
Glistening footprints will forever stay.

With each stride, spirit's warmth does grow,
In the heart of winter, love will glow.
Through every season's ebb and flow,
Let our footprints shine, let life bestow.

Hushed Tales of the Frozen

In the heart of winter's bite,
Silent stories take their flight,
Whispers dance in icy air,
Frozen echoes show they care.

Beneath the snow, the memories sleep,
Ancient voices softly creep,
Tales of love and loss unfold,
In the grasp of frost, so bold.

Moonlight glimmers on the trees,
A soft touch in the chilling breeze,
Every flake a tale to share,
Wrapped in stillness, pure and rare.

As shadows stretch, the sun will rise,
With each dawn, a new surprise,
Frosty whispers fade away,
Yet the stories wish to stay.

In this land, the silence reigns,
Carrying deep, the winter's gains,
Hushed tales murmuring through the frost,
In this beauty, none is lost.

Frost's Gentle Lament

Tenderly the frost does weep,
Crystals in the silence creep,
Pale blue tears on barren ground,
Nature's sigh can be profound.

Each whisper of the freezing night,
Holds a heart, a fading light,
Memories wrapped in icy lace,
Gentle shadows leave their trace.

While the world lies fast asleep,
Frosty promises to keep,
Underneath the stars so bright,
Melody of calm and light.

Bated breath and bated heart,
The early morn, a fresh new start,
Frost recedes, but not its song,
The echoes still, a crystal throng.

Embrace the chill, the quiet we find,
Frost's gentle touch, so soft, so kind,
In each flake, a world concealed,
Nature's tears, lovingly revealed.

The Whispering Pines

Among the pines, a secret stirs,
Gentle winds, like whispered purrs,
Fingers glide on needles green,
Tales of ages lost between.

Frosted branches sway and dance,
In the twilight, shadows prance,
Voices mingling with the night,
Nature's chorus, pure delight.

Each rustle tells a story bold,
Of summers lost and winters cold,
In the hush, a spirit flies,
Through the dark, a soft reprise.

Snowflakes drift on gentle sighs,
With each breath, a truth complies,
Hidden bonds not readily shown,
Inviting hearts to feel at home.

In the sanctuary of the pines,
Within their shade, the world aligns,
Whispering tales of days long passed,
Moments cling, forever cast.

Shadows of a Frosty Dawn

With the break of dawn's first light,
Frosty shadows take their flight,
Glimmers on the glassy ground,
Nature's peace in silence found.

Every corner hooded white,
Echoes soft, a pure delight,
Each breath held in the cool air,
A dance that whispers, unaware.

Shadows stretch across the field,
Secrets of the night revealed,
Birds begin their morning song,
Frosted moments, soft yet strong.

Sunrise paints the world anew,
Casting warmth in every hue,
Yet still, shadows linger near,
Wrapping dawn in crystal cheer.

In the stillness, hearts may yearn,
For the warmth, the light's return,
But in the frost, there lies a grace,
In every shadow's soft embrace.

Hibernation Dreams of the Heart

Whispers of warmth in cold nights,
A fluttering heart, as soft as light.
Beneath the frost, dreams lay still,
Cradled deep, where woods reside.

Silent echoes of time gone by,
Under layers, the soul does sigh.
In the stillness, hope takes flight,
Awaiting spring's gentle kiss, so bright.

Wrapped in layers, we hold our breath,
In nature's pause, there lies no death.
For even frozen, life can hear,
Awakening soon, through the chill and sheer.

Veils of snow shroud past desires,
In slumber's grasp, our heart's sweet fires.
The pulse of life, beneath the freeze,
Stirs softly, like a winter breeze.

As seasons turn, we dream anew,
In hibernation, the heart stays true.
Awaiting warmth, to rise again,
In dreams of love, we'll never wane.

Murmured Secrets in Snowdrifted Silence

Amidst the hush of falling flakes,
Secrets whisper that winter makes.
Glistening snow, a canvas white,
Cradles tales in soft twilight.

Footsteps quiet, the world seems still,
Each drifting thought, a gentle thrill.
Voices linger in frosty air,
Murmurs of love, of sudden care.

Underneath the crystalline veil,
Stories emerge, like a hidden trail.
Echoes dance on a velvet ground,
In snowdrifted silence, secrets abound.

In every flake, a spark of truth,
Memories captured, both old and youth.
With each breath, the cold embraces,
Whispers of joy in silent spaces.

As shadows stretch and daylight fades,
Nature's heart in soft cascades.
We find connection, deep and divine,
In murmured secrets, our souls entwine.

Tracing Footprints in Crystal Powder

In white repose, we leave our marks,
Through crystal powder, nature's sparks.
Each step a story, gentle and bold,
In winter's grasp, our pathways unfold.

With every crunch, the world awakes,
Footprints linger, like whispered flakes.
A journey woven in threads of frost,
Each moment cherished, never lost.

Beneath the blue of winter skies,
We trace the paths where the heart lies.
Treading softly on nature's skin,
Finding solace, where dreams begin.

Each snow-kissed step a dance of grace,
As we wander through this sacred space.
In the quiet, the heart takes flight,
Tracing footsteps, chasing light.

The canvas changes with every breath,
In icy realms, we conquer death.
For in these prints, our essence stays,
Forever etched in winter's praise.

Flickers of Life in Chilly Shadows

Beneath the chill of winter's breath,
Flickers of life defy the death.
In shadowed corners, warmth ignites,
A dance of hope on starry nights.

Amidst the frost, a glimmer shines,
In icy realms, where fate entwines.
The heartbeat soft, beneath the freeze,
Resilience found in whispered pleas.

Each breath a spark, each thought a flame,
Echoes whispering, calling your name.
In darkest hours, light finds a way,
Of flickers of life that choose to stay.

From barren branches to the sky,
Life pushes forth, reaching high.
Though shadows loom, the spirit grows,
In chilly realms, such beauty shows.

Look closely now, see how they play,
Flickers of life that light the way.
In the depth of winter, we shall find,
An ember's glow, forever entwined.

Memories Wrapped in Frozen Breath

Whispers of the past entwine,
Images dance in frost's design.
Snowflakes fall like silent tears,
Each one holds a hint of years.

Footsteps echo through the cold,
Stories waiting to be told.
Embers of joy, shadows of pain,
Fleeting moments, loss and gain.

Time stands still in winter's clutch,
Frozen moments, a gentle touch.
Echoes linger, softly sway,
In the heart, they find their way.

Beneath the ice, the warmth remains,
Cradled deep in hidden veins.
Memories wrap like a warm embrace,
In the stillness, I find my place.

Each breath draws in the silent night,
Wrapped in dreams, soft and light.
Soon will come a thawing sun,
But these memories won't be undone.

Soft Footfalls in a Silent World

In the stillness, whispers glide,
Silent hopes in shadows bide.
Footfalls dance on softened ground,
In this peace, my heart is found.

The trees stand tall, a watchful sight,
Branches bare in pale moonlight.
Each step taken, a gentle grace,
In this moment, I find my space.

Quiet lands where echoes fade,
Nature's canvas, softly laid.
I tread lightly on dreams unmet,
Each soft footfall, a sweet duet.

The night wraps all in velvet dreams,
Stars are stitched in silver seams.
With every breath, I feel the still,
A serene calm, a heart to fill.

In this world where silence reigns,
Joy emerges from whispered strains.
Soft footfalls guide my way anew,
In each heartbeat, I am true.

A Glimpse of Crystal Tranquility

Glistening shards of purest light,
In their presence, all feels right.
Nature's art, a silent sigh,
Whispers of peace drift from the sky.

Through the trees, the sunlight weaves,
Casting spells, as the heart believes.
Each ray dances, a gentle call,
In this moment, I feel it all.

Frozen lakes, like mirrors bright,
Reflect the calm of endless night.
In this gaze, I find my mind,
A glimpse of grace, forever kind.

Clouds drift by in soft embrace,
Time pauses in this sacred space.
Nature's heartbeat, steady and true,
In crystal moments, I renew.

As twilight falls, the world transforms,
In quiet hush, a calm conforms.
A glimpse of peace in beauty's guise,
In tranquility, my spirit lies.

Frosty Kisses of the Morning Sun

Glimmers greet the waking day,
Frosty kisses in morning's play.
Sunlight breaks with tender care,
Each beam dances in the air.

The world adorned in crystal sheen,
Nature's art, a sight serene.
Whispers of warmth begin to rise,
As dawn's soft glow paints the skies.

A golden hue on fields of white,
Transforming frost to pure delight.
With every ray, the chill gives way,
To moments bright, come what may.

Birdsong flutters in the breeze,
Echoing through the waking trees.
Frosty kisses, fleeting yet bold,
In each heartbeat, stories unfold.

With every dawn, new dreams are spun,
In the embrace of morning sun.
Frost melts down, yet love remains,
A tender warmth amid refrains.

Ethereal Frost Patterns

Delicate crystals on glass,
Whispers of winter's art,
Nature's brush, a gentle pass,
Crafting beauty, pure and smart.

Patterns twirl and dance so light,
In the morning's soft embrace,
Sunrise paints them, warm and bright,
A fleeting, enchanted space.

Each flake unique, a star's caress,
Stories told in icy glow,
Eternal moments, we possess,
In frosted time, their beauty flows.

Glistening trails on bark and stone,
Silent witnesses of the cold,
Nature's wonders overgrown,
In winter's hold, they softly mold.

When the thaw begins to break,
Trails of frost will disappear,
Yet in memory, they awake,
The charms of winter, ever near.

Musings in a Frozen World

Windswept whispers in the night,
Each flake dances like a dream,
In this realm of cold delight,
Beauty flickers, shadows gleam.

Footsteps crunch on frozen ground,
Echoes of the past collide,
Silent secrets all around,
Winter's magic, our guide.

Branches draped in crystal lace,
Cascading down, a frozen sigh,
In this wonder, find your place,
Underneath the pale blue sky.

Thoughts drift like the snowflakes fall,
Lightly turning in the air,
In this stillness, we hear the call,
Of a world beyond compare.

As the frost begins to yield,
New life stirs in thawing ground,
Yet in dreams, the snow is sealed,
A frozen world where hope is found.

Frosted Echoes

In the hush of winter's breath,
Echoes linger, soft and clear,
Like a dance of life and death,
Frosted whispers drawing near.

Branches bare beneath the sky,
Veils of white grace every place,
Nature's art we can't deny,
A calm touch, a frozen lace.

Softly falling, without sound,
Mirrored skies in silver gleam,
World wrapped gently all around,
This serene and snowy dream.

Through the haze of chilly light,
Images of past embrace,
Fallen dreams in purest white,
Traces of a hidden place.

When the thawing sun will rise,
Echoes fade but never die,
Frozen tales in heart reside,
Beneath the vast and azure sky.

Silent Snowfall Serenade

Softly drifting down the lane,
Silent notes in crystal air,
Every flake, a sweet refrain,
Winter's serenade so rare.

Shadows dance beneath the moon,
In a hush, the world awaits,
Nature's melody in tune,
Frosty dreams as night sedates.

Footsteps whispered through the night,
Trackless paths where few have been,
Every moment, pure delight,
Lost in winter's silver sheen.

Hold your breath, embrace the chill,
In this tranquil, frozen time,
Feel the magic, feel the thrill,
Listen close, the snow's soft rhyme.

As dawn breaks, the silence fades,
Sunlight bathes the sleeping trees,
Yet the memory gently wades,
Through the heart, with every breeze.

Nightfall's Glacial Caress

The moon spills silver on the ice,
Whispers of night in shadowed skies.
Stars twinkle softly, hush the day,
A world of frost where whispers play.

Blankets of snow, a tranquil sight,
Each flake a gem in the quiet night.
Trees wear crowns of glistening white,
Embraced by cold, a pure delight.

Frozen rivers sing their song,
Underneath the surface, currents strong.
Guided by dreams, we drift and sway,
In nightfall's arms, we're led astray.

The frost-kissed air, a gentle bite,
Wraps us close, in moment's flight.
Around the fire, shadows dance,
In glacial caress, we take a chance.

Beneath the dome of endless space,
We find our hearts in winter's embrace.
With every breath, the world stands still,
In nightfall's grace, we feel the chill.

A Song Beneath the Icy Canopy

In forests deep, the silence grows,
A song that only winter knows.
Each branch a note, each whisper clear,
Beneath the trees, the world feels near.

Crystals hang from every leaf,
A sparkling crown, the heart's belief.
Wind stirs gently through the boughs,
The song of ice, it takes its vows.

Softly woven, branches sway,
In icy arms where shadows play.
Harmonies of night unfold,
A tale of warmth in winter's cold.

The ground is crisp, the night profound,
In stillness, beauty knows no bound.
With every breath, the music swells,
In the canopy, a million bells.

As stars look down, they hum along,
In every flake, we find a song.
In silence deep, we lose the fight,
Beneath the icy canopy, we unite.

Shards of Light on Snow

Morning breaks with softest glow,
Turning white to vibrant show.
Shards of light on snowflakes dance,
Nature's jewels in a silent trance.

Crystalline paths beneath our feet,
Each step a spark, a moment sweet.
Sunrise paints the world anew,
A canvas bright in every hue.

The air is crisp, a fleeting breath,
Whispers of life and lingering death.
In this realm of purest white,
Hope glimmers in the morning light.

Rays filter through the frosty trees,
Carrying dreams on the gentle breeze.
In every corner, beauty flows,
Shards of light where the soft wind blows.

As shadows stretch, the day awakes,
In every nook, the heart now breaks.
With every glance, we come to know,
The magic found in shards of snow.

Whispers of the Icebound Breeze

In twilight's grip, the stillness reigns,
The icebound breeze, it softly gains.
Each whisper carries tales untold,
Secrets buried in winter's hold.

Frozen echoes call our name,
In the wind, we're caught in game.
Branches sway like dancers free,
A ballet born from winter's glee.

Clouds of white drift overhead,
In silence linger, dreams are fed.
The cool embraces every sigh,
Wrapped in whispers where hearts lie.

Moonlight twinkles, casting beams,
Painting softly on frozen streams.
A world transformed in silver light,
Whispers linger through the night.

As dawn approaches, frost retreats,
But in our hearts, the stillness beats.
We cherish whispers, soft and bold,
Of icebound breezes, pure and cold.

Veils of Frosty Light

In the dawn's soft embrace,
Whispers of winter gleam,
Veils of frost gently trace,
A dance in a waking dream.

Beneath the pale morning star,
Shadows stretch and twine,
Nature hums from afar,
In the chill of a silent shrine.

Branches draped in silver lace,
Catch the sun's tender glow,
Time slows in this enchanted space,
As the world breathes low.

Echoes of laughter rise,
In the soft, crisp air,
Each note a soft surprise,
Floating without a care.

In the heart's quiet glow,
Frosty veils dissolve slow,
Revealing warmth we know,
In the light's gentle flow.

Serenade of the Solstice

Underneath the star-clad skies,
A symphony takes flight,
Voices rise, and shadows sigh,
In the solstice's soft light.

Candles flicker in the night,
As secrets softly dance,
Nature's pulse, a steady beat,
In the moon's bold romance.

Winds carry tales from afar,
In whispers, they entwine,
Each note, a guiding star,
In rhythms pure and divine.

The world becomes a stage anew,
Where dreams begin to play,
United in the evening's hue,
As night consumes the day.

As dawn approaches with its glow,
The serenade will fade,
Yet in our hearts, the echoes grow,
Of magic softly made.

Crystal Echoes

In the stillness of the night,
Whispers weave like threads,
Crystal echoes take their flight,
Where silence gently treads.

Mirrored stars in velvet skies,
Glisten, soft and bright,
Echoing our quiet sighs,
In the heart of twilight.

Each moment, a fleeting chance,
To capture dreams so rare,
In the moon's serene romance,
Floating softly through the air.

Fragments of the past, they gleam,
In patterns we can't trace,
Time's elusive, tender dream,
Carved on memory's face.

As dawn breaks the spell we weave,
Crystal echoes dissolve,
Yet in our hearts, we believe,
New melodies evolve.

When Silence Falls

When silence falls like snow,
A blanket soft and white,
The world begins to slow,
In the embrace of night.

Thoughts drift like autumn leaves,
In the stillness profound,
Nature quietly weaves,
In the hush, love is found.

Every heartbeat whispers low,
In shadows softly cast,
A gentle ebb and flow,
Connecting futures past.

Stars blink in distant grace,
As dreams begin to bloom,
In the night's warm embrace,
We find peace amidst gloom.

When silence falls around,
Our spirits begin to rise,
In this sacred ground,
Awakening our skies.

Echoes Beneath the Ice

Whispers drift where shadows lie,
Silent tales of days gone by.
Frozen stillness wraps the night,
Echoes fade, then take to flight.

Underneath the glistening sheet,
Memories stir with quiet beat.
In the depths where secrets dwell,
Frozen dreams cast a gentle spell.

Cracks and creaks, a distant song,
Lifetimes passed, yet time feels wrong.
Cascading thoughts long and wide,
In the ice, where shadows hide.

Moonlight glints on frosted hue,
Shapes of life now lost in blue.
Nature's breath, a fragile sound,
Soften hearts where hopes are found.

Longing hearts entwined with cold,
Dreams arise, yet left untold.
In the echoes, we find peace,
Through the ice, our fears release.

The Call of the North Wind

Whistling through the pines so tall,
Nature's voice, it beckons all.
Chilling breath that sweeps the land,
A steady pulse, a guiding hand.

It carries tales from far and wide,
Adventures known, and hopes inside.
Each gust holds the wisdom old,
Stories wrapped in winds so bold.

Through valleys deep and mountains high,
The North Wind sings a fervent sigh.
In the twilight, shadows blend,
With every breath, the seasons mend.

Let it dance upon your face,
Feel the world in its embrace.
Whispers of the wild roam free,
The call of nature, wild and free.

As night descends, the winds do play,
Carrying dreams both night and day.
In its song, we find our way,
The North Wind's call, come what may.

Celestial Rhapsody

Stars align in cosmic grace,
A symphony in endless space.
Whirling lights with secrets brush,
In the darkness, dreams do hush.

Planets dance in silent tune,
Under guardians of the moon.
Galaxies twist like flowing streams,
In this vastness, we find dreams.

Each twinkle sings a story bold,
Of love and loss, the young and old.
Constellations weave their tales,
Through the night, the magic sails.

Comets trail with fiery glow,
Chasing wishes from below.
Nebulae in colors bright,
Paint the canvas of the night.

In the quiet, hearts take flight,
Lost in rapture, pure delight.
Celestial echoes, soft and sweet,
In their embrace, our souls entreat.

Crystal Bowls of Silence

Empty bowls of crystal clear,
Whispers held, yet so sincere.
In the stillness, secrets lie,
Moments pass, like clouds on high.

Each reflection, a story missed,
Silent echoes in morning mist.
Voices fade into the light,
Leaving traces in the night.

Time's caress upon the glass,
In the quiet, shadows pass.
Thoughts like water gently flow,
In the calm, we come to know.

Serenity in every space,
Capturing the world's embrace.
Glimmers dance on edges fine,
Inviting peace, like vintage wine.

Through the silence, we can hear,
Life's sweet murmur, ever near.
Beneath the bowls, the silence sings,
Of simple joys that living brings.

Lullabies of the North

In the quiet night, whispers flow,
Snowflakes dance soft, a gentle show.
Auroras paint the sky so bright,
Lullabies cradle the winter's light.

A blanket of white on the ground,
Silent dreams in stillness found.
Echoes of peace in frozen air,
Nature hums a timeless prayer.

Winds weave tales from ages past,
Moments of magic, forever to last.
The moon's embrace, a silver glow,
Guiding the tranquil path below.

As stars twinkle in the deep, dark skies,
The heart of the North softly sighs.
Wrapped in wonder, we drift away,
Carried on night's gentle sway.

Each lullaby sings of love's sweet grace,
In every corner, a warm embrace.
Surrender to dreams, let the world rest,
In the North's arms, we are blessed.

Crystalline Hush

Snowflakes gather, a silent choir,
Each a whisper, soft as fire.
In the frosty air, a gentle pause,
Nature's beauty, without cause.

Crystalline hush blankets the land,
A shimmering gift from winter's hand.
Stars blink gently, a celestial dance,
In this stillness, our hearts enhance.

Footsteps muffled, lost in white,
Curled in warmth, away from night.
Breathe in the calm, let worries cease,
In this realm, we find our peace.

Glowing embers in the fireplace,
Draw us closer in this warm space.
The world outside fades from view,
Safety in silence, a moment true.

Crystalline dreams softly arise,
Wrapped in warmth, beneath cold skies.
In this hush, we lose all time,
Within the stillness, we softly rhyme.

Secret Songs of Snowflakes

Snowflakes fall with a secret song,
Each unique, where they belong.
They twirl and glide through chilly air,
Whispers of magic everywhere.

Dancing lightly on winter's breath,
Carving stories with grace, not death.
Each flake tells tales of days gone by,
In the silence, we hear them sigh.

In the moonlight, they shimmer bright,
Casting shadows in the night.
A melody soft, they softly weave,
In their beauty, we believe.

Gathered on branches, a fleeting sight,
Nature's art, pure and white.
In their descent, they speak to souls,
Illuminating the heart's hidden goals.

Listen close to their gentle tune,
Beneath the stars and silver moon.
Secret songs from above, they share,
In whispers cold, with a tender care.

A Stillness in the Air

The world is hushed, in shades of gray,
Winter wraps the earth in its sway.
Trees stand tall, adorned in frost,
In this stillness, nothing is lost.

Breath visible in the chilly night,
Stars above twinkle with delight.
A blanket of silence, deep and wide,
In this calm, we take our stride.

Footsteps echo on the snowy ground,
In the stillness, lost is found.
One with the night, we drift and sway,
In this moment, we long to stay.

Whispers of wind through branches weave,
A tapestry of dreams we believe.
Nature's heart beats soft and slow,
In the stillness, love will grow.

As dawn approaches, colors flare,
Yet in the stillness, we lay bare.
With every breath drawn in the cold,
We find warmth in the stories told.

Nurturing the Silent Night

The moon spills light on velvet skies,
Whispers of dreams in gentle sighs.
Crickets croon a lullaby sweet,
As peace and calm in shadows meet.

Night wraps us in its soft embrace,
Cradling thoughts in a hidden space.
Stars twinkle softly, a watchful eye,
Guarding the world as the hours fly.

In silence, secrets ebb and flow,
Nature's whispers begin to grow.
Like a soft quilt on weary souls,
Night nurtures us, making us whole.

A canvas painted black with grace,
In every corner, a quiet trace.
The stars are stories, each one a spark,
Illuminating the vast, dark park.

So let the night breathe dreams anew,
Underneath skies of deep, dark blue.
In every shadow, hope will light,
Embraced forever, nurturing night.

A Dance of Distant Flakes

In the air, a gentle swirl,
Snowflakes twirl in a winter whirl.
Softly landing, they kiss the ground,
Whispers of beauty, a silent sound.

Each flake unique, a fleeting art,
Crafted with care, each plays its part.
Together they weave a blanket white,
Transforming the world in soft, pure light.

Children giggle, they leap and glide,
With every fall, they spread their pride.
In swirling winds, they dance and play,
A ballet of winter in a frosty ballet.

The trees wear crystals, a regal crown,
While twilight dims, and sun goes down.
Nature's magic unfolds with grace,
A fleeting moment we must embrace.

As darkness falls on this snowy night,
Each flake reflects the silver light.
In a world where stillness takes its stake,
We find our dreams in distant flakes.

The Language of Ice and Silence

Crystals form in the early dawn,
A tapestry woven, the world reborn.
The chill wraps tight, a whisper soft,
In frozen silence, our spirits loft.

Nature speaks in a voice so pure,
Of ancient tales, it does allure.
Each crack and creak, a story unfolds,
In the language of ice, time gently holds.

The rivers freeze, a tranquil sight,
Reflecting stars in the velvet night.
A shimmer of silver, a spark divine,
Each frozen moment is perfectly fine.

Amidst the stillness, we pause to hear,
The echoes of silence, crystal clear.
In every breath, the cold air bites,
But warmth ignites in starry nights.

So listen closely as winter calls,
In icebound dreams, true magic sprawls.
With each soft glance, the heart aligns,
To the language of ice and silent signs.

Shivering Stars Above

In the quiet sky, they shimmer bright,
Stars like diamonds fill the night.
Each twinkle tells a cosmic tale,
Of ancient lore, they softly sail.

Beneath their gaze, we stand in awe,
Wondering at the universe's law.
Whispers of dreams from worlds afar,
Carry the wishes to each shining star.

The night is cold, but our hearts ignite,
In the embrace of soft starlight.
We chase our hopes on beams of gold,
With every heartbeat, stories unfold.

Shivering softly in the frigid air,
The stars beckon us, their light so rare.
In the vast expanse, we find our place,
Connected to the night's warm embrace.

So let us dream under this sky,
With shivering stars, we learn to fly.
With every twinkle, a promise made,
In the universe's dark parade.

The Slumbering Spirit of Cold

A whispering wind in the night,
Silent shadows take flight.
Frosted breath on the glass,
Time seems to slowly pass.

Stars twinkle in a blanket deep,
The world wrapped in a dreaming sleep.
Each flake a story, softly spun,
A tapestry where dreams are won.

Beneath the boughs, the winter sighs,
Nature's secrets in frozen ties.
From branches hang the crystal tears,
Reflecting memories of the years.

The moonlight dances on abyss,
In cold's embrace, there's endless bliss.
A spirit stirs in the night,
Guiding hearts with gentle light.

As dawn breaks with its first gold hue,
Awakens all that frolic anew.
Yet in the cold's soft, tender hold,
Lies the warmth of stories told.

Lullaby of the Snow-Covered Hills

Hills wrapped in a snowy shroud,
Whispers soft, a gentle crowd.
The silence sings a lullaby,
Underneath the vast, clear sky.

Footprints fade in the white expanse,
Nature invites us to a trance.
Each flake whispers tales of old,
A winter magic to behold.

In the stillness, dreams take flight,
Cuddled close in starry night.
The breath of winter, crisp and clear,
Brings forth joy, dispelling fear.

Trees adorned in glistening white,
Holding secrets through the night.
A landscape painted, pure and bright,
Cradled softly in the light.

As shadows lengthen, hearts embrace,
The beauty found in winter's grace.
In the hills, the magic swells,
A lullaby the spirit tells.

The Artistry of Ice-Crystal Dreams

In the morning's soft embrace,
Ice crystals glisten, holding grace.
Each design, a fleeting glance,
Nature's art in winter's dance.

A painter's brush, the frost bestows,
On windows, fields, and wooden bows.
Delicate forms crafted with care,
Frozen memories etched in air.

Light filters through the icy lace,
Casting shadows, a celestial trace.
Each sparkle tells a story bright,
Whispering truths in morning light.

In the stillness, visions wend,
Through dreams where ice and beauty blend.
The artistry of winter's hand,
Binds us gently to this land.

A canvas vast, adorned and free,
Nature's wonders, pure ecstasy.
In each crystal, stories gleam,
The magic of a chilling dream.

The Caress of Chill in the Air

A gentle touch, the icy breeze,
Whispers secrets through the trees.
The world stands still in winter's sway,
Wrapped in arms of white and gray.

Each breath a fog in morning light,
Fleeting moments, pure delight.
The chill caresses cheek and brow,
Awakening the senses now.

Frost-kissed petals greet the morn,
Burdened branches, heavy, worn.
In this season, hearts draw near,
As warmth blooms amidst the fear.

With every gust, the silence grows,
Nature's peace in flakes and snows.
A lull, a hush, a sacred air,
We find solace—nothing compares.

Yet with the cold comes laughter's sound,
In frosty games where joy is found.
The caress of winter's breath,
Reminds us all of life's sweet depth.

Dreams Wrapped in Snowdrifts

Whispers of winter softly call,
Echos of dreams that gently fall.
Wrapped in silence, night's embrace,
Snowdrifts cradle every trace.

Moonlit paths through frosted trees,
Carried away on the evening breeze.
Imagination takes to flight,
In the heart of the winter night.

Blankets of white, a peaceful sight,
Hope wrapped in snow, pure and bright.
Each flake a dream that dances free,
In the realm of fantasy.

Footsteps fade in the sparkling glow,
Lost in the magic of freshly fallen snow.
A world transformed, so calm and still,
Wrapped in dreams, we linger at will.

Time slows down in the chilly air,
Moments frozen, a timeless affair.
Each breath a cloud, soft and light,
Dreams wrapped in snowdrifts take flight.

Secret Stories of the Frost

Under the chill, where silence dwells,
Secret stories the frost compels.
Each crystal formed holds tales unspoken,
Of winter nights and promises broken.

Windows framed with icy lace,
Whispers of warmth in a cold embrace.
Nature's canvas, pristine and clear,
Stories of love, of hope, and fear.

Tracks of creatures across the white,
Sketching secrets in the fading light.
Laughter echoes in the crisp air,
As children weave a dreamlike snare.

The trees stand guard, their branches bare,
Holding memories that linger there.
Each flake a sigh, a gentle breath,
Life and wonder amidst the death.

Beneath the frost, life patiently waits,
To tell its story of love and fates.
In the embrace of winter's sighs,
Secret stories quietly rise.

The Poetry of Frozen Time

Frozen moments caught in flight,
Capturing beauty, soft and white.
A stillness speaks in frozen lines,
Drafts of dreams where time reclines.

Each snowflake is a word well-placed,
In the poetry nature has traced.
Silent verses whisper through the trees,
A sonnet carried on the breeze.

Glittering landscapes, a palette bright,
Scenes of wonder, pure delight.
Each glance reveals a hidden rhyme,
In the soft embrace of frozen time.

Shadows stretch as the day gives in,
While twilight spins its tale within.
Woven stories in the dying light,
Transform the world into pure white.

Moments linger, as if to pause,
Nature's rhythm, the perfect cause.
In every flake a piece of art,
The poetry of frozen time imparts.

Chilled Shadows at Dusk

Dusk drapes shadows across the land,
In chilling whispers, the night takes stand.
Branches sway in the evening air,
Painting pictures of dreams laid bare.

Soft sighs echo through the trees,
Carrying tales on the winter breeze.
Frosted edges glimmer and gleam,
Tales unfold in a twilight dream.

Reflections dance on the whispering snow,
As the world wraps in a soft glow.
Silhouettes linger in fading light,
Creating magic in the night.

With every shadow, a story told,
Of love and warmth in the bitter cold.
Chilled whispers weave through the night,
As dreams awaken, hearts take flight.

Under the stars with hearts aglow,
The essence of winter begins to flow.
Chilled shadows gather, whispers embrace,
A tranquil moment, a sacred space.

Frosted Murmurs

Whispers dance on winter's breath,
Softly spoken, wrapped in zest.
Each crystal spark, a timeless thread,
Frosted dreams where silence wed.

Gentle sighs beneath the night,
Moonlit gleam, a fleeting light.
In shadows deep, the secrets lie,
Winter's hush, a lullaby.

Branches bare, their stories told,
In frosted lace of white and gold.
Echoes drift like distant chime,
Memories caught in chill of time.

Footprints trace along the way,
In frozen fields where children play.
Laughter rings in crisp, clean air,
A timeless joy beyond compare.

Stars peek down on frosty ground,
In this wonder, peace is found.
Nature's song, a sweet refrain,
Frosted murmurs, soft as rain.

Chilling Secrets

In the woods, where shadows creep,
Old tales linger, secrets deep.
Beneath the snow, the stories sleep,
Chilling whispers that we keep.

Frozen echoes softly call,
In the silence, hear them all.
Nature's breath, a ghostly sigh,
Hiding dreams that drift and fly.

Crystalline, the branches sway,
Holding secrets of the day.
As the cold takes hold of night,
Chilling truths emerge in light.

Ancient woods and frosted trees,
Holding mysteries on the breeze.
Each step careful, each glance keen,
In the white, the past is seen.

Here the world seems to stand still,
Frozen moments, hearts can fill.
Chilling secrets softly shared,
In the silence, all prepared.

Frost-Kissed Dreams

As dawn awakens, soft and bright,
Frost-kissed dreams take gentle flight.
In every sparkle, wishes gleam,
Carried high on winter's beam.

Clouds like whispers, drift above,
In this realm we find our love.
Nature's canvas, pure and wide,
Frosted paths where secrets hide.

Snowflakes flutter like a sigh,
In their dance, we learn to fly.
Each flake unique, a magic thread,
Woven stories, softly said.

Through the trees, the sun will peek,
Warming hearts, a gentle tweak.
Frost-kissed dreams, we hold them near,
In winter's grasp, love transcends fear.

As twilight falls, the stars will gleam,
Guiding us through frost-kissed dream.
In this beauty, hand in hand,
Together, we will make our stand.

Silent Snowfall

Softly falls the silent snow,
Blanketing the earth below.
In the quiet, time stands still,
Winter whispers, soft as will.

Each flake unique, a work of art,
Filling gaps in nature's heart.
Like a dream, so pure and white,
Silent snowfall, pure delight.

Footsteps muffled, secrets deep,
In the night, the world does sleep.
Gentle winds weave through the trees,
Carrying the softest pleas.

Stars above, like diamonds shine,
In this moment, all is fine.
Silent snowfall, soft embrace,
A peaceful calm in winter's grace.

As day breaks, colors blend,
Winter's canvas, without end.
In each flake, a chance to dream,
A serenity, a tranquil theme.

Frosty Veils of Serenity

Whispers dance on winter's breath,
Softly blanketing the earth.
A hush that wraps the silent trees,
In crystal dreams, the heart finds peace.

Moonlight glimmers on frozen streams,
Casting shadows and silver beams.
Nature sighs beneath the snow,
In frosty veils, all worries go.

Footsteps crunch on icy ground,
Each echoing the stillness found.
While stars adorn the velvet sky,
In winter's embrace, we wander high.

The world is paused, a tranquil scene,
Laced with frost, a timeless sheen.
Here, in the chill, I'm truly whole,
As serenity envelops my soul.

In this realm, let moments freeze,
Where troubles melt like morning breeze.
Underneath the frosty veil,
In silence, peace will always prevail.

Cold Nights and Warm Hearts

In the glow of fireside light,
We gather 'round on winter nights.
Laughter mingles with breath of steam,
Wrapped in warmth, we share our dreams.

The chill outside might nip and bite,
Yet inside glows our spirits bright.
With stories told and mugs held tight,
We find our joy in the coldest night.

Snowflakes fall like whispered dreams,
Transforming scenes with gentle gleams.
Hearts entwined in cozy circles,
Love ignites through winter's hurdles.

Beneath the stars, the world feels right,
Even as frost whispers its bite.
In every hug, in every cheer,
Cold nights warm hearts, bring us near.

As long as we hold each other dear,
No winter chill will bring us fear.
Together, we'll brave the bitter cold,
In our warmth, life's stories unfold.

The Stillness of Feathered Flurries

Snow softly falls, a soft ballet,
Feas of white in gentle sway.
Silent dancers drift from above,
In the stillness, there's a kind of love.

Each flake is unique, a perfect design,
Creating a canvas, pristine, divine.
Together they settle, a blanket so bright,
Transforming the landscape, pure and white.

Underneath this feathered shower,
Nature holds a quiet power.
Stillness reigns through every tree,
In flurries' flight, I feel so free.

Time seems to pause in this snowy grace,
As winter whispers its soft embrace.
Amongst the silence, I find my peace,
In the feathered flurries, my worries cease.

Nature's art, so calm and slow,
Leaves me in awe as I watch it grow.
With every flake, a gentle sigh,
In the stillness, the world feels high.

Echoes in the Crystal Landscape

In frosted woods where silence reigns,
Echoes whisper through snowy plains.
Footsteps crunch, the sound so clear,
In the crystal landscape, all things dear.

Trees stand tall, adorned in white,
A breathtaking view, pure delight.
The world is wrapped in a frosty glow,
As the winter's beauty starts to show.

Reflecting light, the snowflakes gleam,
Turning the world into a dream.
In frozen splendor, we find our way,
Echoes of joy in this crystal sway.

Breath clouds linger in the air,
Each moment is rare, beyond compare.
Nature's quiet, a gentle embrace,
Wrapped in wonder, we find our place.

In this serene, enchanted land,
Together we walk, hand in hand.
Echoes of laughter fill the space,
In the crystal landscape, we find grace.

Glistening Echoes of the Past

In twilight's glow, the shadows dance,
Whispers of time, lost in a trance.
Memories linger, soft and bright,
Glistening echoes in the night.

Through ancient woods, the stories roam,
Carried by winds, they find their home.
Each leaf a page, each branch a thread,
In the tapestry of what once was said.

With every step, the history calls,
Lost moments trapped within the walls.
Time's gentle touch, a lover's sigh,
Glistening echoes, never to die.

In quiet corners, secrets unfold,
Tales of the brave, the timid, the bold.
A flicker of light in a vast, dark sea,
Reminds us of who we used to be.

So pause and listen, let heartbeats guide,
To glistening echoes where dreams reside.
In the heart of the past, new paths we find,
Connecting the present, forever entwined.

Solitary Stars in Still Nights

In the blanket of night, stars softly gleam,
Solitary jewels, lost in the dream.
Silent sentinels in the velvet sky,
Whispers of wishes, drifting by.

Each twinkle holds secrets of ages gone,
Stories of love, of battles won.
Faint laughter echoes from light-years past,
Through the void, their beauty cast.

Solitude reigns in the vast expanse,
Cosmic ballet, a timeless dance.
They shimmer alone, yet never astray,
Guiding the wanderers, lighting the way.

In the stillness, a moment to breathe,
Finding our place, as we weave and wreathe.
In the dark, we learn to ignite,
Our own shining stars, embracing the night.

So look to the heavens, let dreams take flight,
With each solitary star, we find our light.
In the embrace of the cosmos, we belong,
Woven in stardust, forever strong.

Gentle Hibernation Lullabies

In the quiet woods, where time slows down,
Gentle whispers wear the winter's crown.
Lullabies drift on the frosty air,
Nature's embrace, tender and rare.

Beneath the snow, life softly sleeps,
Dreaming of spring and the promise it keeps.
Blankets of white wrap the earth so tight,
In the cradle of darkness, awaits the light.

Branches bow low with a frosted gleam,
Each breath a puff of a fleeting dream.
Softly they sway, in the cold winds' sigh,
Singing of warmth as the days pass by.

The world slows down in a gentle embrace,
Finding a rhythm, a calming pace.
In hibernation, the heart's lullabies,
Awake in the stillness, a new hope will rise.

So lay down your burdens, in silence confide,
As the earth whispers softly, our worries subside.
In the warmth of rest, let your spirit take flight,
With gentle hibernation, into the night.

Voices from the Frozen Realm

In the land where silence paints the air,
Voices of ice weave tales so rare.
Crystalline echoes, sharp and clear,
Carry the stories that only we hear.

Each flake a memory, frozen in time,
Melodies drift in a haunting rhyme.
Through frostbitten trees, they sway and twirl,
A symphony crafted in a frozen swirl.

The howling winds sing of journeys long,
Of lost wanderers, both weak and strong.
In the frozen realm, they find release,
As the chorus of nature whispers peace.

Through valleys deep and mountains high,
Echoes of whispers in the midnight sky.
A tapestry woven of ice and snow,
Voices resound, in a rhythmic flow.

So listen closely, let your heart unveil,
The hidden notes in winter's tale.
In the frozen realm, a truth we find,
The voice of the earth, forever entwined.

Celestial Heralds of the Icy Night

Stars twinkle bright, a glimmering sight,
Whispers of winter, wrapped in the night.
Moonlight dances on blankets of snow,
Nature's silence sings, a soft, gentle flow.

Frozen breath hangs in the crisp, cold air,
Echoes of laughter, memories we share.
The world's stillness wraps like a cozy shawl,
Under the spell of night's wondrous call.

Trees in their coats, shimmering white,
Guardians of dreams in the heart of the night.
Crystals of frost sparkle on every twig,
As time gently pauses, both humble and big.

Footsteps are muffled, the world feels serene,
In the glow of starlight, a magical scene.
Each breath a cloud, each heartbeat a song,
The beauty of silence, where we all belong.

Celestial heralds, keepers of light,
Guide us through shadows, to warmth from the night.
In the embrace of the winter's soft chill,
We find a soft comfort, the heart's quiet thrill.

The Beauty of Stillness in White

A blanket of white, pure and so bright,
Whispers of snowflakes take graceful flight.
Branches hang low with their frosty adorn,
Nature awakens to the hush of the morn.

Stillness descends like a soft, tender kiss,
Moments of peace, a beautiful bliss.
The world holds its breath in the chill of the air,
Each flake tells a story, unique and rare.

Footprints left soft on the glistening ground,
Echoes of laughter are sweetly profound.
In this frozen canvas, we paint with our hearts,
Creating our memories, where stillness imparts.

Rustling leaves silenced, their whispers now hushed,
The beauty of stillness, in winter, we trust.
A moment to cherish, a pause in the rush,
In the calm of the white, we find our own hush.

The dance of the snowflakes, they twirl and they weave,
In the heart of the cold, there's warmth to believe.
Through every soft flurry, we come to embrace,
The beauty of stillness, winter's sweet grace.

Watching the World Turn to Ice

Glistening surfaces, a mirror-like sheen,
The world transforms with a magical scene.
Rivers and ponds wear a crystalline dress,
In the still of the night, white wonders impress.

Trees stand like statues, adorned with frost,
In this icy realm, nothing feels lost.
Every breath hangs in a delicate mist,
Moments like these, how can we resist?

Nature's sweet silence, a blanket of calm,
Wrapped in the chill, each heartbeat a balm.
Watching the world as it slowly concedes,
To winter's embrace and the beauty it breeds.

The crackle of ice beneath each wandering foot,
Echoes of softness wherever we root.
A miracle unfolds with each shimmering glance,
In the heart of the frost, we find our own dance.

The skies stretch in hues that fade into night,
As we marvel at nature's soft, tender light.
Watching the world, it's a painter's delight,
Transforming our lives as it turns into white.

The Enchantment of Frost-Laden Nights

In the depths of the night, frost whispers and glows,
A tapestry woven with delicate flows.
Stars serenade softly, a shimmering tune,
Embracing the darkness, a magical boon.

Branches adorned in their shimmering coats,
The symphony of cold sings to our hopes.
Through shadows and stillness, enchantments arise,
Mirrored reflections in winter's bright eyes.

Each frosted breath tells a story anew,
In the heart of the night, where dreams come true.
With twinkling crystals that dance in the light,
We bask in the wonder of frost-laden nights.

Silhouettes linger in the silvered moonbeam,
A world wrapped in wonder, as if in a dream.
The hush of the night carries peace like a dove,
In the magic of frost, we discover our love.

The beauty of winter, a canvas so fine,
In the glow of the darkness, our spirits align.
The enchantment of nights with frost gently kissed,
Reminds us of joys that we cannot resist.

www.ingramcontent.com/pod-product-compliance
Ingram Content Group UK Ltd.
Pitfield, Milton Keynes, MK11 3LW, UK
UKHW032216171224
452513UK00010B/482